FOOD LOVERS

GRILLS
& SALADS

FOOD LOVERS

GRILLS
& SALADS

RECIPES SELECTED BY JONNIE LÉGER

Trans
Atlantic
Press

All recipes serve four people,
unless otherwise indicated.

For best results when cooking the recipes in this book, buy fresh ingredients and follow the instructions carefully. Make sure that everything is properly cooked through before serving, particularly any meat and shellfish, and note that as a general rule vulnerable groups such as the very young, elderly people, pregnant women, convalescents and anyone suffering from an illness should avoid dishes that contain raw or lightly cooked eggs.

For all recipes, quantities are given in standard U.S. cups and imperial measures, followed by the metric equivalent. Follow one set or the other, but not a mixture of both because conversions may not be exact. Standard spoon and cup measurements are level and are based on the following:

1 tsp = 5 ml, 1 tbsp = 15 ml, 1 cup = 250 ml / 8 fl oz.

Note that Australian standard tablespoons are 20 ml, so Australian readers should use 3 tsp in place of 1 tbsp when measuring small quantities.

The electric oven temperatures in this book are given for conventional ovens with top and bottom heat. When using a fan oven, the temperature should be decreased by about 20–40°F / 10–20°C – check the oven manufacturer's instruction book for further guidance. The cooking times given should be used as an approximate guideline only.

CONTENTS

BEEF AND VEGETABLE SALAD WITH PEANUTS

Ingredients

500 g /about 1 lb beef sirloin

1 tbsp. oil

8 oz / 250 g carrots, cut into matchsticks

8 oz / 250 g green beans, trimmed

7 oz / 200 g broccoli florets

2 scallions (spring onions), cut into rings

For the dressing:

6 tbsp. lemon juice

6 tbsp. sunflower oil

1 tsp. sesame oil

1 tsp. cane sugar

1 tsp. ginger, finely chopped

1 clove garlic, finely chopped

Salt & freshly ground pepper

In addition:

2/3 cup / 100 g roasted peanuts

1 green chili

Method

Prep and cook time: 50 min

1 Preheat the oven to 325°F (160°C/ Gas Mark 3). Trim the beef. Heat the oil and brown the meat on all sides and then put it into the preheated oven and roast for about 20 minutes. Take out, wrap in aluminum foil and let rest in the oven at a very low heat.

2 Blanch the vegetables (apart from the spring onions) one after the other in boiling, salted water (carrots and broccoli for 4 minutes each, beans for about 8 minutes). When each vegetable has been blanched, take out of the pan, refresh in cold water and drain.

3 For the dressing, mix all the dressing ingredients and season to taste.

4 Mix the prepared salad ingredients with half of the dressing. Wash and trim the chili and cut into thin rings. Slice the beef thinly across the grain and mix lightly with the salad. Arrange on a large platter, sprinkle with the rest of the dressing and scatter with peanuts and chili rings.

PEPPERS WITH COUSCOUS, PINE NUTS AND RAISINS

Ingredients

8 medium red peppers halved lengthwise and seeded (stems intact)

1½ cups / 350 ml chicken broth (stock)

1 pinch saffron threads

½ cup / 100 g raisins

¼ cup (½ stick/ 50 g butter

2 cloves garlic, minced

1 cup / 150 g couscous

1 tbsp curry powder

1½ tsp garam masala*

1 cup / 80 g finely chopped toasted almonds

½ cup / 40 g toasted pine nuts

2 tsp finely chopped shallots

Salt and freshly ground pepper, to taste

8 small bay leaves, stalks attached

Melted butter for basting

For the chili yogurt sauce:

1 cup / 250 g sheep milk yogurt

4 tbsp milk

Juice of ½ lemon

1 pinch chili powder

1 pinch cayenne pepper

½ tsp sweet paprika

Salt, to taste

Method

Prep and cook time: 1 h

1 Preheat the broiler (grill) at low setting.

2 Fill a large bowl with very cold water. Bring a large saucepan of water to a boil. Add the peppers and cook 2-3 minutes; quickly remove them with a slotted spoon to the water to cool. Drain and set aside.

3 Heat the broth (stock) in a saucepan until hot. Add the saffron threads, raisins, butter and garlic and stir briefly, then add the couscous and stir gently. Cover and let stand 30 minutes.

4 Fluff the couscous with a fork and season with curry powder, garam masala, almonds, pine nuts, shallots, salt and pepper.

5 Stuff the peppers with the couscous mixture, using the bay leaf stalks to hold the sides and secure the filling (or use toothpicks). Brush with melted butter and place under the broiler (grill) for about 15 minutes, turning the peppers frequently and brushing them with melted butter.

6 Meanwhile, prepare the yogurt sauce: combine the yogurt, milk, lemon juice, chili powder, cayenne pepper and paprika powder and season with salt.

7 Place the pepper halves onto plates, pour a little yogurt sauce over the top and serve.

*Garam masala, a "warming" spice blend used in Indian cuisine, often contains black pepper, cinnamon, cloves, coriander, cumin, cardamom, fennel and other spices. Find it in Asian groceries and gourmet shops.

SMOKED SALMON AND APPLE SALAD

Ingredients

2 red onions, sliced

2 apples, cored and sliced

4 gherkins, sliced

14 oz / 400 g thinly sliced smoked salmon

2 tbsp pickled green peppercorns

¼ cup oil

½ cup balsamic vinegar

2 tsp honey

Salt and freshly ground pepper, to taste

Method

Prep and cook time: 15 min

1 Gently arrange the sliced onions, apples and gherkins on 4 plates. Lay the smoked salmon slices on top. Sprinkle with peppercorns.

2 In a small bowl, whisk the oil, vinegar and honey to make a vinaigrette; season with salt and pepper and serve with the salad.

CHICKPEA AND SPINACH SALAD

Ingredients

4 tbsp olive oil

2 tbsp cider vinegar

1 tsp medium-hot dry mustard

1 pinch sugar

Salt and freshly ground pepper, to taste

6 cups / 350 g baby spinach leaves

14-oz / 400-g can chickpeas, rinsed and drained

2 beefsteak tomatoes, cored, seeded and diced

1 ripe avocado, pitted and diced

8 plums, pitted and cut into wedges

3 scallions (spring onions), finely chopped

Method

Prep and cook time: 20 min

1 Whisk together the oil, vinegar, mustard and sugar in a large bowl to make a vinaigrette. Season with salt and pepper.

2 Add the spinach, chickpeas, tomatoes, avocado, plums and scallions (spring onions) and toss gently to coat. Divide between four plates and serve.

CHICKEN WITH BACON AND POTATO-WATERCRESS SALAD

Ingredients

For the potato salad:

1¾ lb / 800 g new potatoes, peeled and halved if large

2 tbsp walnut oil

4 tbsp vegetable oil

3 tbsp cider vinegar

1 tsp dry mustard

Salt and freshly ground pepper, to taste

½ bunch scallions (spring onions), thinly sliced

For the chicken:

4 skinless boneless chicken breast, halved lengthwise

Salt and freshly ground pepper, to taste

1 tbsp olive oil

1 tsp butter

4 slices bacon

1 tbsp finely chopped fresh parsley

1 bunch watercress, trimmed

3–4 lettuce leaves, torn into bite-size pieces

Method

Prep and cook time: 50 min

1 Cook the potatoes in boiling salted water until tender, about 25 minutes. Drain and cut into bite-size pieces.

2 Whisk the oils, vinegar, mustard, salt and pepper in a large bowl. Add the potatoes and scallions (spring onions), mix well and let stand to absorb the flavors.

3 Meanwhile, heat the broiler (grill) and season the chicken with salt and pepper. Put under the broiler (grill) and cook thoroughly. Heat the oil and butter in a skillet and fry the bacon until crisp. Take out and drain on paper towels, leaving the fat in the skillet.

4 Arrange the potato salad on plates with the watercress and lettuce, add the chicken and bacon and serve.

AVOCADO AND MOZZARELLA SALAD

Ingredients

2 mozzarella balls

2 ripe avocados

3–4 tbsp. lemon juice

3 scallions (spring onions)

1–2 red chilis, slit open lengthways, deseed and dice finely (wear gloves to avoid irritation)

3–4 tbsp white wine vinegar

2 tsp balsamic vinegar

1 tsp mustard

1 pinch sugar

Salt & freshly milled pepper

4–6 tbsp. olive oil

2–3 tbsp finely shredded basil leaves

Basil leaves, to garnish

Method

Prep and cook time: 15 min

1 Slice the mozzarella. Halve the avocado and remove the pit. Cut the avocado halves into thin wedges, peel and sprinkle immediately with lemon juice.

2 Wash and trim the scallions. Chop the white and light green parts and snip the green tops into rings.

3 Mix the vinegars with the mustard, sugar, salt and pepper and whisk in the oil. Then stir in the finely chopped basil leaves.

4 Arrange the mozzarella and avocado on a large plate, overlapping the slices neatly. Scatter with chili and spring onions and sprinkle with the salad dressing. Serve garnished with basil leaves.

CHICKEN IN SPICY COCONUT

Ingredients

4 chicken breasts

2 cloves garlic, finely chopped

1 chili, sliced (wear gloves to prevent irritation)

1 tsp freshly grated ginger

1¾ cups / 200 ml coconut milk

Zest and juice of 1 lime

Wooden skewers

Sesame oil

Salt & freshly milled pepper

Method

Prep and cook time: 20 min plus Marinating time: 12 h

1 Dice the chicken breasts.

2 Mix the garlic, ginger, chili, coconut milk, lime juice and zest to make a marinade and then mix with the diced chicken. For the best results put into a plastic bag so that everything is well covered and marinate in the refrigerator overnight.

3 Soak the wooden skewers in enough water to cover for 30 minutes (to prevent burning). Preheat the broiler (grill). Take the chicken out of the marinade, thread onto wooden skewers, sprinkle with a little oil and season with salt and pepper. Grill for 4–5 minutes, until cooked, turning occasionally.

SESAME CRUSTED TUNA

Ingredients

1¾ lb / 800 g fresh tuna fillet
(a longish piece)

Salt and freshly ground pepper, to taste

6 tbsp soy sauce, divided

5 oz / 150 g cellophane noodles

1 lb / about 400 g sugar snap peas,
trimmed and halved lengthwise

Juice of 2 limes

1 tbsp fish sauce

1 pinch sugar

1 bunch scallions (spring onions),
thinly sliced along the diagonal

1 bunch cilantro (coriander) leaves,
finely chopped (reserve a few whole
leaves for garnish)

4 hot red chilies, seeded and thinly
sliced (wear gloves to prevent
irritation)

3 tbsp sesame oil

2 tbsp white sesame seeds

2 tbsp black sesame seeds

Method

Prep and cook time: 50 min

1   Season the fish with salt and pepper and sprinkle with 3 tablespoons of the soy sauce. Cover and marinate in the refrigerator 30 minutes.

2   Meanwhile, put the cellophane noodles into a bowl, pour plenty of boiling water over them and let stand until softened, 10 minutes. Drain and cut into shorter lengths with kitchen scissors; set aside.

3   Cook the sugar snap peas in boiling salted water just until bright green, 1-2 minutes; drain in a colander under cold running water to stop cooking. Set aside.

4   Whisk the lime juice, the remaining soy sauce, fish sauce, and sugar in a large bowl; season with salt and pepper. Add the sugar snap peas, scallions (spring onions), cilantro (coriander) and chilies and toss to coat. Add the cellophane noodles and toss gently.

5   Heat the sesame oil in a wok or large skillet. Pat the tuna dry with paper towels and sear quickly on both sides. Roll in sesame seeds and slice thickly.

6   Divide the salad onto plates, add a few slices of tuna to each and garnish with the reserved cilantro (coriander) leaves.

BEAN SALAD WITH ONIONS AND TOMATOES

Ingredients

6 tbsp olive oil

½ cup / 100 ml vegetable broth (stock)

4 tbsp white wine vinegar

½ tsp dry mustard

Salt and freshly ground pepper, to taste

1 pint / 500 g cocktail tomatoes, halved

2 cups / 150 g canned small white beans (eg navy or haricot), rinsed and drained

2 red onions, thinly sliced

Fresh parsley leaves, for garnish

Method

Prep and cook time: 30 min

1 In a medium bowl, whisk the oil, broth, vinegar and mustard to make a vinaigrette; season with salt and pepper.

2 Add the tomatoes, beans and onions and toss to coat. Let stand 20 minutes to marinate.

3 Sprinkle a few parsley leaves over the salad before serving.

NOODLE SALAD WITH SHRIMP

Ingredients

7 oz / 200 g cellophane noodles

2 tbsp vegetable oil, divided

8 jumbo shrimp (king prawns)

1–2 cloves garlic, minced

2 tbsp lime juice, divided

2 eggs, beaten

½ cup / 50 g bean sprouts

1–2 scallions (spring onions), chopped into 2-inch (5-cm) pieces (reserve a few for garnish)

¼ cup chopped roasted peanuts

4 slices pickled red ginger, chopped

1–2 tbsp rice vinegar

Fish sauce, to taste

Chili sauce, to taste

Salt and white pepper, to taste

Method

Prep and cook time: 40 min

1 Put the cellophane noodles into a bowl, pour plenty of boiling water over them and let stand until softened, 10 minutes. Drain. Cut the noodles into smaller lengths.

2 Heat 1 tablespoon of the oil in a wok or skillet and quickly stir-fry the shrimp (prawns) and garlic. Sprinkle with 1 tablespoon lime juice and set aside.

3 Heat the rest of the oil in a small skillet and scramble the eggs.

4 Mix the cellophane noodles with the bean sprouts, scallions (spring onions), scrambled eggs, peanuts and ginger. Divide onto plates.

5 In a small bowl whisk the rice vinegar, the rest of the lime juice, fish sauce, chili sauce, salt and white pepper; sprinkle over the salad. Put the shrimp on top of the salad and garnish with the reserved slivered scallions.

LAMB AND POTATO SALAD

Ingredients

2 red bell peppers, cored and quartered lengthwise

1¼ lb / 600 g potatoes, peeled and quartered

Salt and freshly ground pepper, to taste

6–7 tbsp olive oil

1 tsp curry powder

About 1 lb / 500 g loin of lamb, trimmed of fat

2 tbsp lemon juice

2 tbsp wine vinegar

4 cups / 175 g baby salad greens or spring mix

8 oz / 200 g mini mozzarella balls

Method

Prep and cook time: 45 min

1 Season the potatoes with salt and pepper, scatter them in an oven dish and drizzle with a little olive oil.

2 Preheat the broiler (grill). Line a broiler pan with foil. Place the bell pepper pieces skin-side-up on the pan and broil (grill) until the skin blisters and blackens. Take out, cover with a damp cloth and let cool. Then skin and cut into strips.

3 Season the lamb with salt and pepper and rub with a little of the oil. Put under the hot grill for 3–5 minutes each side, depending on preference and the thickness of the meat. Wrap in foil and set aside.

4 Reduce the temperature to 350°F (180°C / Gas Mark 4) and bake the potatoes for 20-25 minutes, turning occasionally.

5 Mix the curry powder with 3 tablespoons of the oil in a small bowl and brush the mixture onto the potatoes. Continue baking for a further 10 minutes, or until tender.

6 In a large bowl, whisk the remaining 4 tablespoons oil, the lemon juice and vinegar to make a vinaigrette. Add the salad greens and gently toss to coat; season with salt and pepper. Divide between 4 bowls and add the mozzarella. Thinly slice the meat and put on top of the salad with the potatoes. Scatter with the pepper strips and serve at once.

ASPARAGUS AND WATERCRESS SALAD

Ingredients

½ lb / 250 g asparagus, trimmed

8 thin slices bacon, halved

4 tbsp olive oil

1-2 tbsp lemon juice

1 tbsp balsamic vinegar

½ tsp sugar

½ tsp medium-hot dry mustard

½ tsp salt

Freshly ground pepper, to taste

1–2 shallots, finely diced

3 cups / 100 g baby spinach leaves, trimmed

2 cups / 100 g watercress, trimmed

2 medium tomatoes, thinly sliced

About 4 oz / 100 g Parmesan cheese

Method

Prep and cook time: 30 min

1   Cook the asparagus in boiling salted water until bright green but still quite al dente, 5 minutes ; drain in a colander under cold running water to stop cooking.

2   Fry the bacon until crisp in a dry nonstick skillet; drain on paper towels.

3 In a large bowl, whisk the oil, lemon juice, vinegar, sugar, mustard and salt to make a vinaigrette; season with pepper and whisk in the shallots.

4   Add the spinach, watercress, tomatoes and asparagus and gently toss to coat. Divide the salad between 4 plates, top with bacon pieces and shave Parmesan over the salad. Season with ground pepper and serve.

RISONI WITH PESTO, MOZZARELLA AND TOMATOES

Ingredients

2 cups/ 400 g risoni (orzo pasta)

2 oz / 50 g basil

Olive oil

¼ cup / 40 g freshly grated Parmesan cheese

Salt & freshly milled pepper

7 oz / 200 g mozzarella

7 oz / 200 g tomatoes

Method

Prep and cook time: 30 min

1 Cook the risoni in boiling, salted water according to the package instructions until al dente.

2 Pick the basil leaves from their stalks, reserve a few to garnish and purée the rest to a paste with a little olive oil and the Parmesan cheese. Season to taste with salt and pepper.

3 Slice the mozzarella. Wash and halve the tomatoes. Brush the tomatoes and mozzarella with olive oil, season with salt and pepper, and grill for 1–2 minutes each side.

4 Drain the risoni, mix with the basil pesto, and season to taste. Spoon onto plates or into dishes, add mozzarella and tomatoes and serve garnished with basil.

CARIBBEAN STYLE PORK

Ingredients

8 ripe tomatoes

½ ripe mango, pitted and finely chopped

3 tbsp mango juice

2 tbsp snipped chives

6 tbsp olive oil, divided

Hot red pepper sauce, to taste

Salt and freshly ground pepper, to taste

2 tbsp finely chopped basil leaves

1 tbsp finely chopped rosemary leaves

1 tbsp tomato paste (purée)

3 cloves garlic, finely chopped

4 (6-oz / 180 g) boneless pork chops

Method

Prep and cook time: 30 min

1 Fill a large bowl with ice water. Bring a large saucepan of water to a boil. One or two at a time, add the tomatoes and cook 8-10 seconds; quickly remove them with a slotted spoon to the ice water to cool. Repeat with the remaining tomatoes. Drain the tomatoes and slip off the skins. Halve and squeeze out the seeds; finely chop.

2 Combine the chopped tomatoes with the mango, mango juice, snipped chives, 2 tablespoons of the oil, hot pepper sauce, salt and plenty of pepper; set aside.

3 Pre heat the broiler (grill) to medium high. Heat the remaining 4 tablespoons oil in a skillet over medium heat; add the basil, rosemary, tomato paste (purée) and garlic. Cook, stirring, for 1 minute. Add the chops and turn once or twice so that both sides are coated in the tomato-herb mixture. Place the skillet under the broiler (grill). Cook, turning frequently, until juices run barely pink when pierced with a fork, about 10 minutes. Season with salt and plenty of pepper and serve at once with the tomato and mango sauce.

SPICY STRAWBERRY SALAD

Ingredients

2 cups / 200 g watercress, trimmed

1 red onion

5 oz / 150 g feta cheese

2½ cups / 500 g strawberries

3 tbsp balsamic vinegar

2 tbsp olive oil

Salt & freshly ground black pepper

Method

Prep and cook time: 20 mins

1 Peel the onion, cut in half, then chop finely. Break up the feta cheese into small crumbs. Wash and hull the strawberries, pat dry, then cut in half.

2 Mix the balsamic vinegar with the olive oil, salt and pepper. Place the strawberries, watercress and onions in a bowl and toss in the dressing. Season to taste with salt and pepper. Divide onto plates, sprinkle some feta cheese over the top and serve.

MEAT PATTIES WITH ONIONS AND TOMATOES

Ingredients

3 oz / 80 g white bread, crusts removed

1/3 cup / 80 ml milk

1 onion, finely chopped

1 tbsp butter

1¾ cups / 400 g mixed ground meat

2 eggs

1 tbsp hot mustard

1 chili, chopped

1 tsp dried marjoram

2 tbsp chopped fresh parsley

Breadcrumbs

Salt & freshly milled pepper

Oil, for brushing

4 tomatoes, quartered

2 red onions, cut into thick rings

Herbs, to garnish

Method

Prep and cook time: 30 min

1 For the meat patties, soak the bread in the milk. Heat the butter in a skillet and sauté the onion over a low heat until translucent.

2 Mix the ground meat with the soaked bread, eggs, mustard, chili, and onion. Add the marjoram and parsley and as many breadcrumbs as necessary to produce a shapeable mixture. Season with salt and pepper.

3 Shape into patties, brush with oil, and grill for 2–3 minutes each side. Sprinkle the red onions and tomatoes with a little oil and put on the grill with the patties.

4 Put the meat patties on plates with the tomatoes and onions. Garnish with herbs and serve with boiled new potatoes.

APPLE AND BLUE CHEESE SALAD

Ingredients

4 apples, cut into wedges

Juice of 1 lemon

1 tbsp butter

1 onion, finely chopped

50 g /2 oz sliced bacon

1 tbsp honey

2 oz / 50 g blue cheese, crumbled

Method

Prep and cook time: 25 min

1 Preheat the grill or broiler.

2 Sprinkle the apple wedges with lemon juice and grill on all sides for 5-6 minutes.

3 Heat the butter in a medium skillet; add the onion and briefly sauté. Add the bacon and fry until golden brown.

4 Divide the apples onto plates and drizzle with the honey. Sprinkle with the bacon-onion mixture and serve scattered with crumbled cheese.

MOROCCAN CHICKEN WITH COUSCOUS

Ingredients

Around 2 lb / 1 kg chicken breast fillets

2 cloves garlic, finely chopped

1 lemon

4 tbsp olive oil

Salt & freshly milled pepper

2–3 tsp Moroccan spice mixture

For the yogurt dip:

1 cup / 250 ml whole-milk yogurt

Salt

1 pinch Moroccan spice mixture:
paprika, cumin, turmeric, ground
coriander , cayenne pepper and saffron

For the couscous:

1 bunch cilantro (coriander)

1¼ cups / 250 g couscous

1 lemon

7 oz / 200 g ripe tomatoes, chopped

1 onion, finely chopped

1 small eggplant (aubergine), diced

1½ red bell peppers, deseeded and diced

Freshly milled pepper

1 tbsp olive oil

2 tbsp white wine vinegar

Method

Prep and cook time: 50 min plus Marinating time: 3 h

1 Remove any skin or fat from the meat. Cut the meat into 12 long thin strips. Wash the lemon, remove the zest with a zester and chop finely. Squeeze the lemon and reserve the juice.

2 Mix 2 tbsp lemon juice and 2 tbsp olive oil with the garlic, half of the lemon zest, salt, pepper, and the Moroccan spice mixture. Add the chicken, mix well, cover, and marinate in the refrigerator for about 3 hours.

3 Mix the yogurt and add the spices and salt to taste. Soak the wooden skewers in enough water to cover for 30 minutes (to prevent burning).

4 Cook the couscous according to the package instructions.

5 Squeeze the lemon and put the juice into a bowl. Add the vegetables to the lemon juice in the bowl.

6 Heat the oil in a skillet, add the mixed vegetables and sauté until they are softened. Stir in the vinegar and mix the vegetables with the couscous along with the cilantro. Check the seasoning.

7 Preheat the broiler (grill). Thread the pieces of chicken on wooden skewers. Sprinkle the chicken with the rest of the oil and broil (grill) on all sides.

8 Spoon the couscous onto plates or into dishes, add chicken skewers and a little yogurt sauce to each and serve.

TURKEY AND PEACH KEBABS

Ingredients

1 lb 4 oz / 600 g skinless boneless turkey breast, cut into bite-size chunks

2 peaches, pitted and diced

1 red bell pepper, cut into bite-size pieces

Vegetable oil, for brushing

1 tbsp oil

1 small chili pepper, chopped (wear gloves to prevent irritation)

1 clove garlic, chopped

1 mango, pitted and finely chopped

1 tsp honey

Light soy sauce, to taste

Fish sauce, to taste

Sea salt, to taste

Hot red pepper flakes, to taste

Method
Prep and cook time: 30 min

1 Preheat the grill or broiler. Soak 8 wooden skewers in water to cover for at least 30 minutes (to prevent burning).

2 Thread the turkey, peaches and bell pepper pieces onto the skewers, alternating them as you go. Brush with oil and grill, turning frequently, 6-8 minutes. Set aside and keep warm.

3 Meanwhile, to prepare the dip, heat the oil in a small skillet, add the chili and garlic and sauté briefly. Add the mango and honey and a little water; bring to a boil and cook, scraping browned bits from the skillet. Add soy sauce and fish sauce to taste and remove from the heat.

4 Put the turkey and peach skewers on plates, drizzle with a little of the dip and sprinkle with salt and pepper flakes. Serve the dip separately in small bowls.

GRILLED ENDIVES WITH TOMATOES

Ingredients

4 endives (heads of chicory)

Juice of 1 lemon

Olive oil

1 lb / 500 g tomatoes

Salt & freshly milled pepper

Fresh marjoram, to garnish

Method

Prep and cook time: 25 min

1 Wash, trim, and halve the endives. Sprinkle with half of the lemon juice, brush with olive oil, and season with salt and pepper. Grill on both sides for 5–6 minutes.

2 Wash and slice the tomatoes and mix with the rest of the lemon juice and 3 tbsp olive oil.

3 Season to taste with salt and pepper and arrange on a platter. Sprinkle with marjoram.

4 Arrange the endives on the other half of the platter and serve.

HALIBUT WITH MANGO AND LIME SALSA

Ingredients

4 (5-6 oz / 150 g) halibut fillets

Salt and freshly ground pepper, to taste

Juice of 3 limes, divided

1 tbsp butter

2 ripe mangos, finely diced

4 tbsp mango juice

1 tsp brown sugar

1 pinch cayenne pepper

1 tbsp chopped cilantro (coriander); reserve a few leaves to garnish

1 lime, thinly sliced, to garnish

1 lemon, thinly sliced, to garnish

Method

Prep and cook time: 30 min

1 Preheat the grill or broiler.

2 Season the fish with salt and pepper and sprinkle each with 1 tablespoon of the lime juice. Grill or broil the fish on both sides for 5-6 minutes.

3 Meanwhile, heat the butter in a skillet over medium heat and add the diced mango. Briefly sauté, then stir in the remaining lime juice and mango juice and season to taste with salt, brown sugar and cayenne. Add the cilantro (coriander).

4 Put the fish onto plates with the mango-lime sauce and serve garnished with slices of lime and lemon and cilantro leaves.

TOMATO SLICES WITH CAPERS AND LEMON ZEST

Ingredients

2 lb / 1 kg plum tomatoes

1 tsp sugar

Sea salt & freshly milled pepper

Olive oil

½ lemon

Some caper berries

Method

Prep and cook time: 15 min

1 Wash the tomatoes, remove the stalks, and cut into thick slices. Sprinkle sugar, salt, and freshly milled pepper over the top.

2 Wash the lemon, remove the zest with a zester and chop finely, and collect the juice in a cup.

3 Drizzle olive oil over the top. Place the tomatoes in a hot grill pan for about 1 minute each side. Remove and arrange onto plates. Drizzle lemon juice over the top, garnish with lemon zest and caper berries, and serve.

STEAK WITH MOZZARELLA AND GRAPEFRUIT

Ingredients

1 grapefruit

2 avocados

4 (5-6-oz / about 160-g) steaks, (e. g. rib eye or sirloin)

4 tbsp olive oil, divided

1 pint / 400 g cherry tomatoes

8 mild red chili peppers

1 clove garlic, minced

About 1 lb / 400 g mini mozzarella balls, drained

Sea salt and freshly ground black pepper, to taste

Method

Prep and cook time: 40 min

1 Turn the broiler (grill) to high.

2 Peel the grapefruit and remove the segments, avoiding the pith and membrane, reserving the juice. Peel and halve the avocados, remove the pits and roughly dice the flesh. Sprinkle with half of the grapefruit juice.

3 Pat dry the steaks, rub them with a little of the oil and place under the broiler (grill). Cook for 3–5 minutes on each side depending on preference and the thickness of the meat. Wrap the meat in foil and set aside.

4 Return the skillet to the heat and sauté the tomatoes, chilies and garlic until softened. Add the remaining grapefruit juice, remove from the heat and add the avocado, mozzarella and grapefruit segments. Toss to combine and season to taste with salt and pepper.

5 Season the meat with salt and pepper. Cut each piece in halves or thirds and put on warmed plates. Add the vegetables and mozzarella and serve.

GRILLED LAMB CUTLETS WITH HERB BUTTER

Ingredients

2 tomatoes, chopped

2 cloves garlic

8 tbsp olive oil

1 tsp freshly chopped thyme

1 tsp freshly chopped rosemary

Salt & freshly milled pepper

12 lamb cutlets, French trimmed, each weighing about 3 oz / 80 g

Tomato wedges, to garnish

Rosemary, to garnish

For the herb butter:

1/3 cup / 2/3 stick / 75 g soft butter

Salt & freshly milled pepper

1–2 tbsp finely chopped herbs:
parsley, chervil, tarragon

1 tsp lemon juice

1 clove garlic, finely chopped

Method

Prep and cook time: 20 min plus Marinating time: 12 h

1 Mix the oil with the herbs, garlic, and chopped tomatoes and season with salt and pepper.

2 Wash and dry the lamb cutlets, put into the tomatoa and garlic marinade, cover and marinate overnight, turning once.

3 Cream the butter with the salt and pepper and mix with the herbs and lemon juice. Peel the garlic, press into the butter and stir in.

4 Shape the butter into a roll, wrap in aluminum foil and chill.

5 Heat the broiler (grill). Drain the lamb cutlets and cook on the hot grill for 2–3 minutes each side.

6 Sprinkle with marinade, arrange on plates and garnish with tomato wedges and rosemary. Add a few slices of the herb butter and serve.

TOMATO AND BEAN SALAD

Ingredients

4 tbsp canned white beans (eg navy or cannellini), washed and drained

4 tbsp fresh broad beans, double podded (outer gray/green skin removed)

1 bunch arugula (rocket)

1 red onion, diced

1 clove garlic, finely chopped

1 vine with tomatoes

¾ cup / 125 g cherry tomatoes

2 tbsp. olive oil

2 tbsp. balsamic vinegar

1–2 tbsp. lemon juice

Salt & freshly milled black pepper

1 pinch sugar

4 ciabatta rolls

Method

Prep and cook time: 1 h

1 Wash the vine tomatoes, cut in half, remove the stalks and seeds, then finely dice. Wash the cherry tomatoes.

2 Sauté the garlic in the olive oil, add the beans and cherry tomatoes and sauté, then remove from the heat and let cool. Now add the onions and the diced vine tomatoes and pour in the balsamic vinegar and lemon juice. Season to taste with salt, pepper and sugar. Let the beans marinate for about 30 minutes.

3 Cut the ciabatta rolls in half and place under the broiler (grill) until golden brown. Spoon some of the bean and tomato salad over the top, garnish with a few arugula (rocket) leaves and serve.

CHICKEN ON STIR-FRIED VEGETABLES

Ingredients

1–2 tsp Chinese five-spice powder

2 limes

12–14 tbsp dark soy sauce

4 chicken breast fillets

11 oz / 300 g snow peas (mangetout), trimmed

1 medium sized zucchini (courgette), sliced

7 oz / 200 g carrots, peeled and cut into matchsticks

2 tbsp oil

½ tsp chili powder

Salt

Scant ½ cup / 100 ml vegetable broth (stock)

3–4 oz / 75–100 g pea sprouts (or bean sprouts if unavailable)

2 tbsp sesame seeds (toasted)

Method

Prep and cook time: 40 min

1 Wash the lime, remove the zest with a zester and chop finely and squeeze the lime. Mix the five-spice powder, the zest and juice of the limes, and 6–8 tbsps. of the soy sauce to make a marinade; marinate the chicken for about 15 minutes.

2 Broil (grill) the chicken under a medium heat until cooked through, for 3–5 minutes on each side (depending on thickness).

3 Meanwhile, heat the oil in a wok. Add the snow peas (mangetout) and stir-fry for 1 minute. Add the zucchini (courgettes) and carrots and cook for a further 2 minutes. Add the chili powder, 2 tbsp soy sauce, and salt. Then add the broth (stock) and cook for a further 5 minutes.

4 Wash and drain the pea sprouts and add to the vegetables with the sesame seeds. Stir-fry for a further 2 minutes.

5 Slice the chicken and drizzle with the remaining soy sauce (or to taste). Serve the stir-fried vegetables onto plates and put the chicken on top.

VEGETABLE PATTIES WITH TOMATO SAUCE

Ingredients

For the vegetable patties:

14 oz / 400 g cauliflower, chopped finely

1¼ lb/ 600 g boiling (waxy) potatoes, peeled and grated

2 eggs

1 tbsp parsley, chopped

1–2 tbsp flour

Salt & freshly milled pepper

Nutmeg

Breadcrumbs, to coat

For the tomato sauce:

1 shallot, finely chopped

1 clove garlic, finely chopped

2 tbsp olive oil

1 tbsp tomato paste (purée)

14 oz / 400 g can chopped tomatoes

Salt & freshly milled black pepper

Method

Prep and cook time: 1 h

1 To make the vegetable cakes, mix the potatoes and cauliflower with the eggs, parsley and flour until combined and easy to form. Season to taste with salt, pepper, and nutmeg. Form the dough into small patties and roll in the breadcrumbs until coated.

2 For the tomato sauce: sauté the shallot and garlic in hot oil, then stir in the tomato paste (purée) and add the chopped tomatoes. Add a little water if required. Simmer gently for about 10 minutes. Purée with a hand blender and season with salt and pepper.

3 Place the vegetable patties under a hot broiler (grill) until golden brown, turning occasionally.

4 Arrange onto plates, drizzle tomato sauce over the top and serve.

CARROT AND TUNA SALAD

Ingredients

About 1 lb / 500 g carrots, peeled and coursely grated

6 oz / 200 g can of water-packed tuna

6–8 tbsp olive oil

4 tbsp wine vinegar

2 tbsp coarse Dijon mustard

2 tsp green peppercorns

3–4 tbsp lemon juice

Lemon wedges, to garnish

Cilantro (coriander), to garnish

Method

Prep and cook time: 25 min

1 Drain and flake the tuna. Mix the tuna with the carrots and put on plates.

2 For the dressing, put the vinegar, lemon juice and Dijon mustard into a container and blend in the oil, adding it in a trickle. Finally mix in the peppercorns and sprinkle the dressing over the salad. Serve garnished with lemon wedges and cilantro (coriander).

MOROCCAN LAMB KEBABS WITH YOGURT SAUCE

Ingredients

1 lb 12 oz / 800 g lamb, from the leg

3 oz/ 80 g mixed salad leaves

4 pita breads

1 lemon

8 wooden skewers

For the marinade:

Juice of 1 lemon

3–4 tbsp olive oil

2 sprigs rosemary, roughly chopped

½ inch / 1 cm fresh ginger, freshly grated

1 pinch cumin

1 chili pepper, finely chopped

For the yogurt sauce:

1 clove garlic

1 bunch parsley, roughly chopped

14 oz/ / 400 g natural yogurt

1 tsp lemon zest

Salt & white pepper

Method

Prep and cook time: 15 min plus Marinating time: 2 h

1 Mix all the marinade ingredients and put into a freezer bag.

2 Cut the meat into ¾ inch (2 cm) cubes and put into the freezer bag with the marinade. Seal and knead to make sure the meat is coated in the marinade. Put into the refrigerator and leave for at least 2 hours. Soak the wooden skewers in enough water to cover for 30 minutes (to prevent burning).

3 For the yogurt sauce, peel and press the garlic. Put into a bowl with the rest of the sauce ingredients and mix thoroughly. Season with salt and pepper. Chill in the refrigerator.

4 Heat the broiler (grill). Take the meat out of the marinade and thread on the wooden skewers. Broil (grill) on all sides for 5–7 minutes. Meanwhile, fold the pita breads and briefly toast/warm them. Cut the lemon into 8 wedges.

5 Arrange the kebabs on plates with the pita bread. Garnish with salad and sprinkle with yogurt sauce. The remaining sauce can be served separately.

APPLE AND CELERIAC SALAD

Ingredients

3 cups / 400–500 g celeriac

3–4 apples

3 tbsp lemon juice

2 sprigs parsley or celeriac leaves

1¼ cups / 300 g low-fat yogurt

Salt & pepper

1 pinch sugar

Brown bread, for serving

Method

Prep and cook time: 20 min

1 Peel and wash the celeriac and cut into slices. Cook in boiling, salted water for about 3 minutes. Drain, place immediately into cold water, then drain again.

2 Peel and quarter the apples and remove the core. Cut into thin slices. Drizzle lemon juice over the apples. Cut the slices of celeriac into thin sticks and mix with the apples.

3 Wash the parsley (or celeriac leaves) and shake dry. Cut into thin strips.

4 Season the yoghurt with salt, pepper, and a pinch of sugar, then add to the apple and celeriac and stir well. Season to taste with salt and pepper. Divide into bowls, sprinkle the parsley (or celeriac leaves) over the top and serve with a few slices of brown bread.

STUFFED BELL PEPPERS

Ingredients

4 red and yellow bell peppers

7 oz / 200 g sheep's milk cheese, chopped

16 red and yellow cherry tomatoes, halved

1 bunch basil, roughly chopped

Salt & freshly milled pepper

2 tbsp olive oil

2 tbsp lemon juice

1 lemon

Method

Prep and cook time: 20 min

1 Halve the bell peppers lengthways, remove the cores, and wash and dry the pepper halves.

2 Mix the cheese, tomatoes, and basil, season with salt and pepper, and stir in the oil and lemon juice. Stuff the bell pepper halves with the mixture and secure with toothpicks. Grill on a hot grill (on a piece of aluminum foil if necessary) for about 5 minutes.

3 Serve garnished with lemon wedges.

MARINATED VEGETABLES

Ingredients

1 lb / 500 g green asparagus

10 oz / 400 g tomatoes, quartered

2 red onions, cut into wedges

Olive oil

Balsamic vinegar

Salt & freshly milled pepper

Parmesan cheese, freshly grated

½ cup / 50 g black olives

Method

Prep and cook time: 30 min

1 Peel the lower third of each asparagus stalk. Blanch in boiling, salted water for about 15 minutes, drain, then place immediately into cold water and drain again.

2 Fry the asparagus, tomatoes, and onions in olive oil in a hot grill pan for about 2–3 minutes.

3 Remove from the pan, drizzle balsamic vinegar and olive oil over the top. Season with salt and pepper and let cool.

4 Sprinkle Parmesan cheese over the top, garnish with olives, and serve.

CHICKEN WITH LIME BUTTER

Ingredients

12 oz / 350 g carrots, sliced

7 oz / 200 g snow peas (mangetout), trimmed

2 cloves garlic

2 tbsp lime juice

1 tsp lime zest

1/3 cup / 2/3 stick / 80 g soft butter

4 chicken breast fillets (skinned)

Salt & freshly milled pepper

Some basil leaves, shredded

Lime slices, to garnish

Method

Prep and cook time: 30 min

1 Blanch the carrots in boiling, salted water for 3–4 minutes, then drain, refresh in cold water, and drain thoroughly.

2 Peel the garlic. Mix the lime juice and zest with ¼ cup (½ stick / 50 g) of the butter. Crush the garlic into the butter and season with a little salt. Mix well.

3 Season the chicken with salt and pepper. Put into a baking dish and spread with the garlic and lime butter. Cook under a preheated broiler (grill) for 5–10 minutes each side.

4 To serve, heat the vegetables in the rest of the butter and season with salt and pepper. Scatter the vegetables with basil and put on plates with the chicken breasts. Serve at once, garnished with lime slices.

SPICY NOODLE SALAD

Ingredients

1 carrot

1 cucumber

2 shallots

½ cup /50 g bean sprouts

3 red chilis

7 oz / 200 g rice noodles

Cilantro (coriander) and mint leaves, shredded

For the Nuoc Cham Sauce:

5 cloves garlic, chopped very finely

5 red chilis, deseeded and chopped very finely

3½ tbsp Vietnamese fish sauce

Scant ½ cup / 100 ml water

3½ tbsp rice vinegar

¼ cup / 50 g sugar

Juice of 1 large lemon

Method

Prep and cook time: 25 min

1 Peel and halve the carrot and cucumber. Remove the cucumber seeds, cut the cucumber in half and cut lengthways into long, very thin strips. Cut the carrot into long very thin sticks. Peel the shallots and slice thinly. Wash and drain the soybean sprouts. Wash, halve and deseed the chilis and cut into rings. Reserve a couple of chili rings to garnish.

2 Cook the noodles in boiling, salted water for about 2 minutes. Then drain, refresh in cold water and drain thoroughly. Set aside.

3 For the sauce, put all the ingredients apart from the lemon juice into a pan and heat, but do not let it boil. Then remove from heat and let cool. Stir in the lemon juice when the sauce is cold.

4 Put the noodles, cucumber, carrots, shallots, chilies and 6 tbsp of Nuoc Cham sauce into a large bowl and mix. Serve on plates, sprinkled with herbs and the reserved chili rings.

SWORDFISH AND TOMATO KEBABS

Ingredients

1½ lb / 600 g swordfish

2 cups / 600 g cherry tomatoes

1 cup / 200 g kumquats, cut into quarters

1 lemon, untreated

2 cloves garlic, finely chopped

½ bunch fresh parsley, finely chopped

Some fresh bay leaves

6 tbsp olive oil

Salt & freshly milled pepper

2 cups / 150 g green lettuce

salt & freshly milled pepper

8 wooden skewers

Method

Prep and cook time: 30 min plus Marinating time: 2 h

1 Soak 8 wooden skewers in water to cover for about 30 minutes (to prevent burning). Wash the swordfish, pat dry, and cut into cubes. Wash the lemon, remove the zest with a zester and chop finely. Squeeze the lemon and reserve the juice in a cup.

2 Thread the fish, tomatoes, bay leaves, and kumquats onto the skewers, alternating as you go. Mix the lemon zest with the garlic, parsley, and four tablespoons of olive oil. Marinate the fish kebabs for about two hours.

3 Remove the kebabs from the marinade, season with salt and pepper, and place under a broiler (grill) for about 3–4 minutes, turning occasionally.

4 Wash the lettuce and break into bite-sized pieces. Arrange the lettuce onto plates. Drizzle the remaining olive oil and the lemon juice over the top and season with salt and pepper. Place two kebabs on each plate, drizzle some of the marinating oil over the top, and serve.

GRILLED GREEN ASPARAGUS WITH EGG SAUCE

Ingredients

about 3 lb / 1½ kg green asparagus

2 tsp salt

2 tbsp oil

For the sauce:

scant ½ cup / 100 ml vegetable broth (stock)

⅓ cup / 75 g /crème fraîche

1 tbsp butter

1 bunch parsley,

2 hard-boiled eggs

1 tbsp capers

Lemon juice

Method

Prep and cook time: 30 min

1 Peel the lower third of each asparagus spear, cut off the ends and cook in boiling, salted water for about 8 minutes, until al dente. Then take out of the water and drain well.

2 Put the vegetable broth (stock), crème fraîche and butter into a pan and simmer over a medium heat until reduced to a slightly creamy consistency. Chop the parsley leaves finely and stir into the sauce. Shell and chop the eggs and stir into the sauce with the capers. Season with salt and pepper and add lemon juice to taste.

3 Brush the asparagus with oil and (broil) grill on all sides on a hot grill for 3–4 minutes. Season with pepper and a little salt and serve on plates with the egg sauce.

GRILLED SHRIMP AND SCALLOP

Ingredients

4 large shrimp (or prawns), deveined and peeled

4 medium scallops

1 stalk lemongrass

2 tbsp lemon juice

1 good pinch saffron threads, crumbled

4 tbsp olive oil

2 cloves garlic, minced

Salt and freshly ground pepper, to taste

4 small red chilies

About 4 oz / 100 g cellophane noodles

2 tbsp vegetable oil

2 scallions (spring onions), thinly sliced on the diagonal

1–2 tbsp dry white wine

1 good pinch turmeric

1 head baby bok choy, quartered

Method

Prep and cook time: 40 min

1 Preheat the grill. Quarter the lemongrass stalk lengthwise and thread 1 shrimp (or prawn) and 1 scallop onto each piece.

2 In a small bowl, combine the olive oil, lemon juice, garlic and saffron threads; season with salt and pepper. Brush the skewers and the chilies with the marinade and grill, turning and brushing frequently with the marinade, 3-4 minutes.

3 Cook the noodles according to the package instructions; drain and set aside.

4 Meanwhile, heat the oil in a skillet and add the scallions (spring onions); sauté briefly. Add the wine and turmeric; bring to a boil, scraping up browned bits from the skillet, and cook until the scallions are glazed. Set aside and season with salt and pepper.

5 Place a bok choy piece on each of 4 plates. Add the noodles and sprinkle with scallions. Place a shrimp and scallop skewer and a chili on top and serve.

LAMB PATTIES IN PITA BREAD

Ingredients

1 small bread roll, stale

About 1 lb / 500 g ground lamb

½ small bunch (1 oz / 25 g) fresh mint leaves, finely chopped (reserve a few whole leaves for garnish)

1 egg

2 oz / 50 g feta cheese, crumbled

1 clove garlic, minced

Salt and freshly ground pepper, to taste

1 good pinch cumin

4 tbsp vegetable oil

2 beefsteak tomatoes

6 lettuce leaves, torn into bite-size pieces

6 pita (pitta) breads, warmed in the oven, split to form pockets

½ red onion, sliced into rings

Method

Prep and cook time: 30 min

1 Place the bread in a large bowl and add enough water to cover; soak briefly, then squeeze out the water.

2 Discard the water in the bowl and add the lamb, soaked bread, chopped mint, egg, feta, garlic, salt, pepper and cumin; mix well to combine.

3 With moistened hands shape the ground meat mixture into six patties. Heat the oil in a skillet and fry the patties, turning once, until no longer pink inside, 6-10 minutes.

4 Meanwhile, slice the tomatoes in half and squeeze out the seeds; finely chop. Combine the lettuce with the reserved mint leaves. Line the pita pockets with half of the lettuce, onions and tomatoes.

5 Place the patties in the pita (pitta) bread pockets and tuck the remaining lettuce and mint leaves around them. Season with salt and pepper and serve at once.

SMOKED CHICKEN AND COUSCOUS SALAD

Ingredients

1½ cups / 250 g couscous

2 tbsp butter

3 cups / 350 g arugula (rocket)

1 small cucumber, sliced

1 radicchio lettuce, torn into bite-size pieces

1 red bell pepper, finely diced

12 oz / 350 g smoked chicken breast

Some fresh basil

Salad dressing

Salt & pepper

Method

Prep and cook time: 30 min

1 Pour hot water over the couscous as instructed on the packet, cover and let stand. Add the butter. Stir through the couscous with a fork and let cool.

2 Mix all the ingredients with the couscous and serve onto plates. Slice the smoked chicken breast and arrange on the salad. Put a spoonful of salad dressing on each. Shred the basil and scatter over the salad. Season with salt and pepper and serve.

MACKEREL WITH HERBS

Ingredients

4 whole mackerel (scaled and gutted, each about 14 oz / 400 g)

Salt and freshly ground pepper, to taste

7 tbsp/ 100 g butter, softened

Juice of 1 lemon

2 tbsp chopped mixed herbs, such as parsley, chervil and/or dill

2 cloves garlic, minced

½ red chili pepper, seeded and finely chopped (wear gloves to prevent irritation)

Method

Prep and cook time: 30 min

1 Preheat the broiler (grill) to a low heat.

2 Fillet the mackerel (or ask the fish merchant to do it for you) and season with salt and pepper. Cut 4 large pieces of foil and place one mackerel fillet on each.

3 Combine the butter with the lemon juice, garlic, chili and herbs, garlic and chile in a bowl. Spread on the fish fillets.

4 Fold the foil around the fish to make open parcels and broil (grill) the fish in the parcels for about 20 minutes (turning once), until the fish is firm and flakes with a fork.

ASPARAGUS AND MUSHROOM SALAD

Ingredients

12 asparagus spears, trimmed

2–3 tbsp butter

1 lb / 500 g brown button (chestnut) mushrooms, sliced

1–1½ red bell peppers, sliced into strips

About 1 cup / 100 g arugula (rocket) leaves

For the dressing:

Zest and juice from 2–3 oranges

4 tbsp vegetable oil

2 tbsp white balsamic vinegar

2–3 tbsp grainy mustard

1–2 tsp honey

Method

Prep and cook time: 30 min

1 Bring a large pot of salted water to a boil; add the asparagus and cook until al dente, about 8 minutes. Drain in a colander under cold running water to stop cooking; set aside.

2 Heat the butter in a skillet; add the mushrooms and sauté until they release and reabsorb their juices. Season with salt and pepper and set aside.

3 Prepare the dressing: in a small jar or salad dressing shaker, combine the orange juice and zest, oil, vinegar, mustard, honey, salt and pepper; shake vigorously to blend.

4 Gently toss the asparagus, bell pepper, and mushrooms with the dressing and add the arugula (rocket). Arrange attractively on plates and serve at once.

SPAGHETTI WITH GRILLED VEGETABLES

Ingredients

14 oz / 400 g spaghetti

1 1/4 lb / 600 g tomatoes

1 clove garlic, finely chopped

Olive oil

1 dash red wine

1 tbsp sesame seeds

Salt & freshly milled pepper

1 eggplant (aubergine), sliced

1 green zucchini (courgette), sliced

1 yellow zucchini (courgette), sliced

1 tsp dried thyme

2 tbsp freshly grated Parmesan cheese

Rosemary, to garnish

Method

Prep and cook time: 40 min

1 Cook the spaghetti according to the package instructions until al dente.

2 Meanwhile, drop the tomatoes into boiling water for a few seconds, refresh in cold water, then skin, quarter, deseed, and chop.

3 Heat 2 tablespoons oil and sauté the garlic, then add a little red wine and the chopped tomatoes. Remove from the heat, add the sesame seeds, and season to taste with salt and pepper.

4 Sprinkle the eggplant and zucchini with olive oil and thyme and season with salt and pepper. Put on a grill and cook for 1–2 minutes each side.

5 Drain the spaghetti, mix with the tomatoes and put into warmed bowls. Add a slice of each vegetable and sprinkle with 1 tablespoon Parmesan cheese. Serve garnished with rosemary. Sprinkle the rest of the vegetables with the remaining Parmesan and serve separately.

GRILLED PEARS WITH SWEET RICOTTA CREAM

Ingredients

2 pears

4 tbsp lemon juice, divided

½ cup / 100 g ricotta

4 tbsp honey, divided

Ground cinnamon, to garnish

Chocolate curls, to garnish

Mint leaves, to garnish

Method

Prep and cook time: 20 min

1 Preheat the grill or broiler.

2 Peel pears if desired; quarter and core. Brush with 2 tablespoons of the lemon juice and grill cut-side down until browned, 2–3 minutes.

3 Meanwhile, in a small bowl, mix the ricotta smoothly with 2 tablespoons of the honey and the remaining lemon juice.

4 To serve, put two pear quarters on each plate, spoon a little ricotta over each and drizzle with the rest of the honey. Dust with cinnamon and scatter with chocolate curls and mint leaves.

GRILLED PEACHES WITH AMARETTI BUTTER

Ingredients

1 egg yolk

1/8 cup / 30 g sugar

1 good pinch ground cinnamon

Scant 1/2 cup /100 ml light cream

3–4 oz / 80–100 g amaretti cookies

1/4 cup (1/2 stick / 50 g) butter, softened

6 firm ripe peaches

1 tbsp sunflower oil

Method

Prep and cook time: 30 min, plus 3 h freezing time

1 Line a baking sheet or tray with foil or parchment.

2 In a large bowl, beat the egg yolk with the sugar for 10 minutes, until pale and creamy. Mix in the cinnamon.

3 In a separate bowl, whip the cream until stiff and fold into the mixture. Shape into 2-tablespoon portions and arrange on the prepared baking sheet; freeze until firm, about 3 hours.

4 Preheat the broiler (grill). Using 3 sheets of foil, shape small "bowls" large enough to hold three peach halves and brush each with a little oil.

5 Put the amaretti into a zip-close plastic bag; seal, squeezing out air. Crush to fine crumbs with a rolling pin. Then combine with the butter and rub together to form coarse crumbs.

6 Place three peach halves in each foil dish with the cut surface facing up; sprinkle with amaretti crumbs. Place on a baking sheet and broil (grill) until soft, about 5 minutes.

7 Put the peaches with their juices onto plates, add a portion of ice cream and drizzle with a little of the juice.

PINEAPPLE SKEWERS

Ingredients

1 pineapple

4 tbsp butter

4 tbsp honey

1 tbsp lemon juice

1 pinch ground cinnamon

1 pinch ground cloves

1/3 cup / 8 cl dark rum

Method

Prep and cook time: 15 mins

1 Soak 8 wooden skewers in enough water to cover for 30 minutes (to prevent burning). Preheat the grill.

2 Cut off the top and bottom end of the pineapple. Stand the pineapple on its end and cut off the peel in strips from top to bottom with a sharp knife. Then cut the pineapple into quarters lengthwise, trim off the hard core from each piece and cut the remaining fruit lengthwise into slices/wedges. Thread onto the skewers.

3 In a small skillet, melt the butter and stir in the honey, lemon juice, cinnamon and cloves; keep warm. Grill the pineapple skewers, brushing with the butter mixture and turning frequently, until evenly browned.

4 Take the skewers off the grill, put into a shallow skillet and pour the warmed rum over. Heat until the rum bubbles, then ignite with a long-handled match or kitchen lighter. Shake the pan gently until the flames subside. Serve at once.

Published by Transatlantic Press

First published in 2010

Transatlantic Press
38 Copthorne Road, Croxley Green, Hertfordshire WD3 4AQ

© Transatlantic Press

Images and Recipes by StockFood © The Food Image Agency

Recipes selected by Jonnie Léger, StockFood

A catalogue record for this book is available from the British Library.

ISBN 978-1-907176-31-9

Printed in China